DON'T STEP ON THE SPIDER

AUTHOR
KIRK RAEBER

CO-AUTHOR
MARK GRAHAM

ILLUSTRATOR
MARC ZAPATA

Jamul, CA
Honey Rock View Publishing

Copyright © 2020 by Kirk Raeber.

All rights reserved. No part of this publication may be reproduced, distributed or transmitted in any form or by any means, including photocopying, recording, or other electronic or mechanical methods, without the prior written permission of the publisher, except in the case of brief quotations embodied in critical reviews and certain other noncommercial uses permitted by copyright law.

Kirk Raeber/Honey Rock View Publishing, Jamul, CA
Printed in the United States of America
Contact:

This is a work of fiction. Names, characters, places, and incidents are a product of the author's imagination. Locales and public names are sometimes used for atmospheric purposes. Any resemblance to actual people, living or dead, or to businesses, companies, events, institutions, or locales is completely coincidental.

Don't Step on the Spider/Kirk Raeber -- 1st ed.

LCCN: 2020900713

ISBN 978-0-9972638-7-9 Print Edition
ISBN 978-0-9972638-3-1 Ebook Edition

Dedicated to the reader

Liam and Olivia
Enjoy the story and message
From your loving Father

"One child, one teacher, one book,
one pen can change the world."

— **Malala Yousafzai**

It is a warm summer day with cotton-white clouds in the sky. Six-year-old Tim sits on the floor of his grandparents' house, playing a video game while Grandma Maria stirs the kettle on the stove and Grandpa Don sits in his favorite chair, reading a book.

Tim jumps up and says, "I'm going outside to play."

"Okay, have fun," his grandfather says.

The front screen door slams, and Tim hurries out. Suddenly he calls out, "Wow, you should see this, Grandpa. Come quick."

Grandpa Don closes his book, winks at his wife, and goes outside. He sees Tim looking at a large spider walking on a beautiful spider web. Tim is about to step on the spider when Grandpa Don calls out, "Don't, Tim. Don't step on the spider."

"But why? It's just a spider." Tim looks puzzled.

"All life is important. Not just people. All life is important," Grandpa Don answers. When he sees the look of wonder on Tim's face, he says, "Come with me. I will show you many different creatures that are a part of our living world."

Grandpa Don pulls out his magnifying glass. He and Tim crouch over the spider and his web. "Meet Legs the spider. Legs, this is my grandson, Tim."

"Hello, Tim," Legs says. "What do you think of my web?"

Tim looks through the magnifying glass and says, "Wow, that is the most amazing spider web I've ever seen."

Grandpa Don winks at Legs and says, "I'm going to introduce Tim to some of our friends. See you around," and off into the woods they go.

"There," Grandpa Don calls, pointing excitedly to a meadow alive with blooming flowers and plants of all types. They walk to a patch of ferns with broad leaves and see a caterpillar sunning herself on a leaf. They bend down with the magnifying glass and find the caterpillar smiling up at them. "Tim, meet my good friend, Kat."

"Well, well," Kat says, stretching her body toward her visitors. "So this is your grandson. A good-looking boy."

"Takes after his grandpa."

"She talks!" Tim says with his eyes wide, hardly believing his ears.

"Oh, I do more than talk," Kat assures him. "I've been eating all summer long preparing for my cocoon, so I can transform into a beautiful new creature," Kat tells Tim.

"Like my friends here." Kat gestures to the many butterflies flying from flower to flower. One of them, a beautiful yellow and gold color, lands on the tip of Tim's nose and stares into his eyes with a wide smile. "You do think I'm beautiful, don't you?" she says.

"I've never seen a butterfly as beautiful as you are," he answers. "I'm Tim. What's your name?"

"You can call me Madame." She winks at Tim, and then flutters back to the flowers.

"Madame and all of her butterfly friends are busy pollinating flowers, so the flowers can make seeds and create food for people and animals," Grandpa explains. "A very important function in our world, Tim. We need caterpillars and butterflies, and they need us."

Tim says, "I would never hurt a butterfly or a caterpillar."

"Okay, then, let's see what else we can find."

The two walk a little further into the woods and spot a large ant hill in an open pasture. They see
streams of ants going in every direction.

"Ants!" Tim calls out.

"Oh, yes," Grandpa says. "Some of our most industrious and important friends!"

"Friends? Ants?"

"Friends indeed," a serious voice says from someplace near their feet. Tim freezes and Grandpa Don chuckles. They look down at a small red ant carrying a very large piece of dirt on his back.

"Well hello there," Grandpa Don says. "Tim, meet Atlas the ant. Atlas, this is my grandson."

"Well, well, well." Atlas drops his dirt and holds out one of his many legs. Tim bends down and shakes it, using his pinkie finger. "How do you do, young man."

"Good, thank you. I'm learning a lot today," Tim replies.

"I was just telling Tim how important you are, Atlas."

"You can say that again," Atlas says. "We are not only one of the strongest creatures on earth given our size, Tim, but also one of the most earth-friendly."

"Earth-friendly? How so?" Tim asks.

"Lots of ways. First, we build tunnels that make the soil healthier so that food can grow. Then we help water and air get to the roots of plants and make them strong. We also take seeds down into the ground where they can sprout and grow and become healthy plants."

"Wow!" Tim's eyes grow wide with admiration. But before he can say anything else, Atlas lifts the large piece of dirt onto his back and joins his fellow ants. Tim and Grandpa Don watch them disappear inside the ant hill.

"Work, work, work," Grandpa says. He puts a hand on Tim's shoulder. "I guess we'd better get out of the way."

Tim and Grandpa pause for a moment to watch a flock of geese flying overhead, then cross the road and stop in the shade of a tall oak tree. Grandpa invites Tim to kneel down in a patch of lush groundcover.

"I don't see anything," Tim says.

"Not everyone lives aboveground, you know," Grandpa says, as he begins digging into the loose soil. Suddenly, two large eyes appear in the dirt, and Grandpa laughs. "Ah, there you are, my wiggly friend. Come on out. I want to introduce you to someone."

Behind the eyes is a long, plump worm. "And who might this be?" Wiggle says, eyeing Tim.

"Say hello to my grandson, Tim. He is learning a thing or two about Mother Nature," Grandpa says. "And how is your family, Wiggle?"

Wiggle the worm gives a low whistle and four other worms wiggle toward them, three of them small and perky. "We were busy fertilizing this very healthy soil until you two showed up."

Tim laughs. "Hello there," he says to the three baby worms.

"Good to meet you," all three say in harmony. "We'd shake your hand if we had hands."

They all laugh. Then his grandpa says, "Our earth wouldn't be as healthy as it is without our good friends the worms, Tim. Never forget that, okay?"

"I won't, Grandpa," Tim says, waving to the worms as they burrow back into the soil. "Bye, guys."

The path leads them between two towering maple trees and a patch of sunflowers.

Tim skips ahead and stops to admire the sunflowers, when all of a sudden, a bright red ladybug with black dots lands on his arm. Tim holds his breath. He turns slowly and whispers, "Grandpa! Look! Right here on my arm!"

Grandpa says, "No need to whisper; this is Lucy, a ladybug. Maybe the most beautiful of all insects. Right, Lucy?"

"No maybe about it," Lucy says, moving from Tim's arm to his nose and gazing into his eyes. "So, count yourself lucky, young man."

Tim smiles. "Oh, I do. I do."

"In fact," his grandpa says, "some people think ladybugs are a sign of good luck. I just think they make the world beautiful."

"Not to mention protecting your crops from a bunch of crop-eating critters," Lucy reminds him.

"Yes, indeed," Grandpa says. "For which we are very thankful. Right, Tim?"

"Right!" Tim calls as Lucy dashes away. "And I promise not to forget."

"Wow," Tim says as they come to a field filled with thousands of bright sunflowers. "So cool."

"Yes," Grandpa Don says with a nod. "Mother Nature sure has a way with color, doesn't she?"

The closer they get to the sunflowers, the more bees they see. "Boy, are they busy," Tim says. "Don't tell me you have a friend here, Grandpa? I sure don't want to get stung."

"You won't get stung if you don't interrupt," a voice calls from one of the yellow blossoms. Sure enough, it is one of the bees.

"That's Buzz," Grandpa says.

Buzz is flying from flower to flower and is too busy to stop. "Don't mean to be rude, but we've got lots of pollinating to do," Buzz calls, giving Tim a wink.

"What's pollinating?" Tim asks as Buzz moves from sunflower to sunflower, his wings buzzing.

"It's nature's way of fertilizing plants so they can produce food," Grandpa says, "so the world has fruits and vegetables to feed humans just like you and me, and birds and bears and hundreds of other animals. We could never survive without the help of bees, Tim."

Tim watches in amazement. "I was always afraid of bees, but now, well, I think I love them."

"Me too," Grandpa says, taking Tim's hand and continuing their tour.

The two come to a small lake surrounded by cattails and long grass. Fish swim in the water and birds fly along the shore.

"Tim! Look there!" Grandpa Don points to a bright blue-green insect with large wings and bright eyes, buzzing back and forth in the tall grass.

"What is it?" Tim says. "I've never seen an insect like this."

"That is Matilda, a dragonfly. Give her a wave. Maybe she'll come over."

Tim waves, "Hello, Matilda."

Matilda looks over when she hears her name and flies straight at Tim. He jumps back. "Hello, Don," Matilda says, her wings buzzing. "Who's the little guy?"

"This is my grandson, Tim." Grandpa Don grins.

"Didn't mean to spook you, Tim, but that's what people expect us to do. Spook them," Matilda says.

Tim moves closer, his eyes wide. "You're beautiful, Matilda," he says.

"The Japanese think dragonflies are symbols of strength, courage, and happiness," Grandpa Don says. "I just think they're fun to watch."

"What your grandpa didn't mention is that we eat mosquitoes, which means there are a lot less of them to bite you," Matilda says. Matilda flies around Tim's head for moment, then back to the lake, and disappears.

"Wow!" Tim says.

"Wow is right," Grandpa agrees. "It's getting dark. We should head back."

Grandpa Don doesn't seem to be in a hurry. He watches the great orange sun setting on the horizon.

"One of my favorite times of the day," he says with a sigh.

"Shouldn't we get going, Grandpa?" Tim asks. "How will we find our way home in the dark?"

His grandpa chuckles and wraps his arm around Tim's shoulder. "I forgot to tell you. I have one more friend to introduce to you. See that?"

All of a sudden Tim sees a small light coming right toward them, followed by many other lights. "Holy cow!" Tim says as the glow of light grows around them.

One of the lights lands on Grandpa Don's hand, and he says, "Well, well, well. If it isn't my very good friend Flash, a firefly."

Flash looks over at Tim, who is now surrounded by dozens of fireflies, all circling around. Tim laughs at this magical sight.

"You two are out pretty late," Flash says. "Why don't my friends and I guide you home?"

"I was hoping you would say that," Grandpa Don replies. "Tim's grandma is probably getting worried."

"Onward," Flash calls, and all of his fellow fireflies gather together and form a beautiful circle of light. They all head back down the path. When they arrive at the house, Grandma Maria is waiting for them on the porch.

"I see you have an escort," Grandma says with a smile.

"The best possible escort," Grandpa says.

"This is Flash and his friends," Tim says. Tim looks at the fireflies and says, "Thank you, guys. That was fun."

"Sleep well," Flash says. "We'll pay you a visit tomorrow night too."

The fireflies disappear into the night, and Tim and Grandpa give Grandma a hug. "I want to hear all about your adventure," she says.

The dinner table is already set, so Tim and Grandpa Don sit down. Grandma Maria brings them dinner. "So, where have you two been all day?"

"Oh, Grandma, it was the best day," Tim says excitedly. "I met so many friends and learned so many things. Did you know that butterflies and bees pollinate flowers so that the world has more fruits and vegetables?"

"Is that so?" Grandma says with a grin. "That's wonderful."

"Worms and ants help make the soil healthy so that our plants can grow and feed the world."

"We could never do without them," she says, winking at Grandpa Don.

"No way," Tim says, munching on a mouthful of broccoli. "And then there is Lucy, she eats other insects that want to destroy our crops. Lucy is so pretty."

"Don't forget to tell her about Matilda," Grandpa says, sipping a glass of milk.

"Matilda is spooky but beautiful." Tim is so excited. "Flash and his friends light up the night! What a cool guy."

"I saw that," Grandma says with awe in her voice. "Like magic."

"But my favorite is Legs. I almost stepped on him earlier and feel terrible about that." Tim sets down his fork. "But we're friends now."

Which character is your favorite? Why?

What did you learn after reading the story?

How will you act when you see the characters in real life?

How are the characters important to our world?

Will you read more books in the future?

Acknowledgments

Writing a children's book is so much different than other types of fiction but just as enjoyable. I would like to acknowledge a number of people who have given me such good comments while writing this book.

Sally Burgarin introduced me to Marc Zapata who is a wonderful illustrator. I am so happy Sally and I talked years ago about who was going to do the illustrations. Sally has been very helpful from an artist stand point in evaluating the drawings and also with the text.

Faith Beltran gave me her invaluable insight into how children would view the story. I made several important changes in the story because of her suggestions.

I am extremely grateful to Julia Bussie, Pete Mishky, Mel Ochs, Ginger Ochs, Gresham Bayne, Patricia Bossano and Marsha Raeber for all their valuable suggestions and advice. Mel Ochs advice about punctuation and the tense of the story was so helpful.

The other beta readers Monique Devoe, Deirdre Brennan, Shannon Carter, Genia Kyres, Jim Kyres and Rachel Nafis with her three boys were so helpful in keeping me focused.

Marc Zapata is a very talented Illustrator who has done a wonderful job drawing the characters for the book. I really appreciate all his hard work and feel he has a bright future ahead of him.

I want to thank Linda Raeber for her encouragement and support.

Colin Graham at Graham Publishing Group has always been accessible to me. I appreciate his extensive knowledge and expertise in the self-publishing environment.

Lastly I could not have written this book without the help of my co-author Mark Graham. Mark is an established author who has written a number of very good novels. I appreciate his friendship and assistance with "Don't Step on the Spider".

AUTHOR
KIRK RAEBER

CO-AUTHOR
MARK GRAHAM

ILLUSTRATOR
MARC ZAPATA

Kirk Raeber is a retired emergency room physician. His first award winning novel is a historical fiction "*Forgotten Letters* ". Kirk decided to change the genre for this book and experience a different adventure. He lives in California with his wife and Anatolian Shepherds.
Contact:
raeberkirk@gmail.com

Mr. Graham is a critically acclaimed author who has been writing and editing professionally since 1988. He has written and published four critically acclaimed full-length novels.

Marc Zapata is a self taught illustrator who has been drawing for over 15 years. He is to expand his work with illustrations, character design and even animation. Marc is truly passionate about art.

Made in the USA
San Bernardino, CA
27 January 2020